D0286944

My husband said he needed more space, so I locked him outside

REFLECTIONS ON LIFE BY WOMEN

Compiled and edited by Cynthia Walker McCullough

A Fireside Book
Published by Simon & Schuster

F

FIRESIDE
Rockefeller Center
1230 Avenue of the Americas
New York, NY 10020

Copyright © 1998 by Cynthia Walker McCullough
All rights reserved,
including the right of reproduction
in whole or in part in any form.

FIRESIDE and colophon are registered trademarks
of Simon & Schuster Inc.

Designed by
Cynthia Walker McCullough & APPLEPRESS

Manufactured in the United States of America

1 3 5 7 9 10 8 6 4 2

Library of Congress Cataloging-in-Publication Data
is available.

ISBN 0-684-84189-4

ACKNOWLEDGMENTS

Without my women friends, our common experience, and shared laughter, this book would not exist.

Special thanks to: my mother, who, with her ever present camera, taught me that a picture is worth a thousand words; my sister, Sharon Bristol, who allowed me to use our images and encouraged me to compile this book; my daughter, Kim, who endures the mother-daughter dance and always teaches me something new; Peter and Alexander, whose specialness takes the "step" out of stepson; Roger Harris and Karen Howard, who taught me the meaning of friendship; Robin Grant-Hall, who in many ways made this book possible; Bob and Ann Bell and my new sister Peggy; Perri Ardman, my friend and sometime creative collaborator, whose images appear in this book; Barbara Brewster, Janice Casal, Judy Colt, Jane Duquette, Phyllis Ostrovsky, and Suzanne Wilson, all good friends; Arnold Skolnick, my friend and creative partner; Larry Lorber, whose friendship and professionalism are invaluable; and Anita Thomas, my valued assistant, who defines the word loyalty.

I want to thank Jack Appelman and Paul Wheeler for their ongoing support and Betsy Radin-Herman of Simon & Schuster for her belief in this book.

A very special thanks to Roseanne, who makes her point with laughter and whose joke became the inspiration for the title of this book.

Finally, I want to thank the people who shared their history and their images: Alan J. Arrowsmith, Lynne Arrowsmith, Barbara Beardsley-Millecam, Dr. Ron Cherubino, Linda Roney Gregory, Helen M. Lisle, Richard Klein, David Roney, Susan Scott, Gloria Simons, Mildred and Joseph Stambovsky, and Phillip and Mark Stambovsky.

With deep gratitude I wish to acknowledge all the women whose quotes, eloquently and with humor, give voice to the basic truths and experiences of our world.

—C.W.M.

For David and Mark
with laughter and love

INTRODUCTION

Many of the pictures in this book represent my personal and family history. Yet they are far more than that. They are snapshots of a generation that read with Dick and Jane, played with Silly Putty and Mr. Potato Head, and greeted the electronic age via a box with a small screen and a black-and-white picture. Through the "miracle" of television, we grew up with Howdy Doody and Buffalo Bob; Kukla, Fran, and Ollie; Uncle Miltie; and Lucy and Ricky. Our images of family life came from *The Donna Reed Show*, *Father Knows Best*, and *The Adventures of Ozzie and Harriet*. (I always wondered why my mother didn't wear pearls and high heels to do the laundry—until I began doing laundry myself years later.)

The quotes in this book come from women of different eras yet have a timeless quality. In researching this book, I found that men were quoted far more frequently than women. Yet, we have warmth, humor, a unique perspective on life, and something to say.

It is my hope that this book will allow people to look back with nostalgia, laughter, and a real sense of shared experience that brought us to the place we are today—the beginning of the second half of our lives.

No sooner had I learned to tell time
than I began arriving late everywhere.

JANE WAGNER

I require only three things in a man:
he must be handsome, ruthless, and stupid.

DOROTHY PARKER

One more drink and
I'll be under the hose.

DOROTHY PARKER
(ADAPTATION OF QUOTE)

It goes without saying that you should never have more children than you have car windows.

ERMA BOMBECK

*L*ead me not into temptation;
I can find the way myself.

RITA MAE BROWN

Cherish forever what makes you unique, 'cuz you're really a yawn if it goes.

BETTE MIDLER

If I had my life to live over again,
I'd dare to make more mistakes next time.

NADINE STAIR

Ask him the time, and he'll tell you how his watch was made.

JANE WYMAN ON
RONALD REAGAN

Laugh and the world laughs with you;
snore and you sleep alone.

MRS. PATRICK CAMPBELL

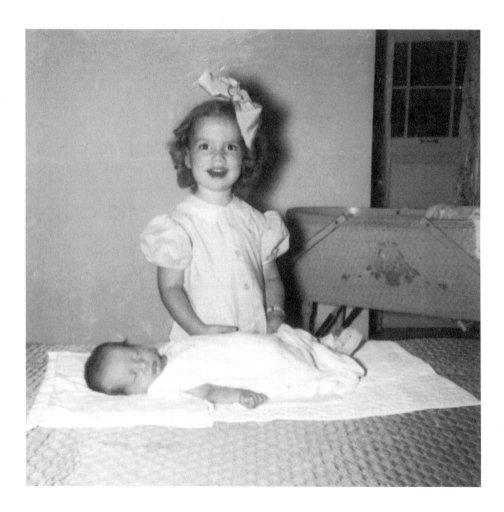

*What should I do when
the world seems upside down?*

C. WALKER MCCULLOUGH

કે

*The average man is more interested
in a woman who is interested in him
than he is in a woman with beautiful legs.*

MARLENE DIETRICH

Children reinvent your world for you.

SUSAN SARANDON

I base most of my fashion taste on what doesn't itch.

GILDA RADNER

If the world were a logical place,
men would ride sidesaddle.

RITA MAE BROWN

When Mom *found my diaphragm,*
I told her it was a bathing cap for my cat.

LIZ WINSTON

*I have bursts of being a lady,
but it doesn't last long.*

SHELLEY WINTERS

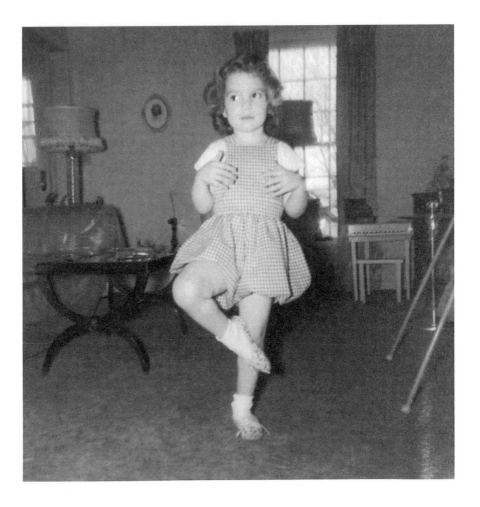

As long as you know
that most men are like children,
you know everything.

COCO CHANEL

Your life story would not make a good book.
Don't even try.

FRAN LEBOWITZ

I never hated a man enough
to give his diamonds back.

ZSA ZSA GABOR

My grandmother started walking
five miles a day when she was sixty.
She's ninety-three today and we
don't know where the hell she is.

ELLEN DEGENERES

Instant gratification takes too long.

CARRIE FISHER

O_h, I'm so inadequate—
and I love myself!

MEG RYAN

I am not a gourmet chick.

PEARL BAILEY

If you don't want your children to hear what you're saying, pretend you're talking to them.

E. C. McKenzie

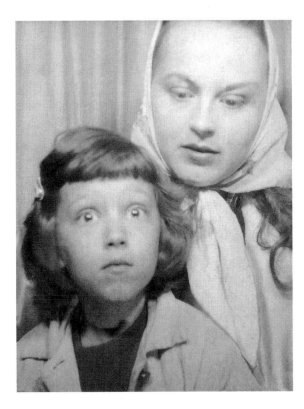

*Everything you see
I owe to spaghetti.*

SOPHIA LOREN

If love is the answer, could you please rephrase the question.

LILY TOMLIN

The girl speaks eighteen languages and can't say no in any of them.

DOROTHY PARKER

*He has a first-rate mind
until he makes it up.*

LADY VIOLET BONHAM CARTER

Good girls go to heaven,
bad girls go everywhere.

HELEN GURLEY BROWN

I'm as pure as the driven slush.

TALLULAH BANKHEAD

No matter how lovesick a woman is, she shouldn't take the first pill that comes along.

DR. JOYCE BROTHERS

The happiest women,
like the happiest nations,
have no history.

GEORGE ELIOT
(MARY ANN EVANS)

❧

If only we'd stop trying
to be happy, we'd have
a pretty good time.

EDITH WHARTON

If God wanted us to bend over,
he'd put diamonds on the floor.

JOAN RIVERS

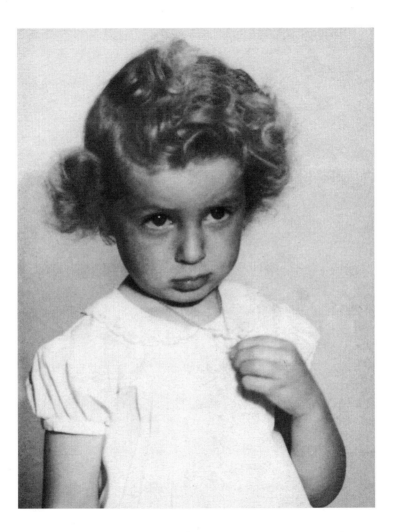

*L*ove conquers all things
except poverty and toothache.

MAE WEST

*Freud is the father of psychoanalysis.
It has no mother.*

GERMAINE GREER

The average girl would rather have beauty than brains because she knows that the average man can see much better than he can think.

LADIES' HOME JOURNAL, 1947

My *favorite animal is steak.*

Fran Lebowitz

*Love is the history of a woman's life,
it is an episode in man's.*

MADAME DE STAËL

Your family are the people
most likely to give you the flu.

JANE WAGNER

*I have often wished I had time
to cultivate modesty…
But I am too busy
thinking about myself.*

EDITH SITWELL

I do not believe in God;
I believe in cashmere.

                    FRAN LEBOWITZ

In passing, also, I would like to say that the first time Adam had a chance, he laid the blame on a woman.

NANCY ASTOR

The trouble with the rat race is that
even if you win, you're still a rat.

LILY TOMLIN

The quickest way to know a woman
is to go shopping with her.

MARCELENE COX

Whenever you want to marry someone,
go have lunch with his ex-wife.

SHELLEY WINTERS

If *you are all wrapped up in yourself,*
you are overdressed.

KATE HALVERSON

We are always the same age inside.

GERTRUDE STEIN

My mother buried three husbands…
and two of them were only napping.

RITA RUDNER

Why does a woman work
for ten years to change
a man's habits and then complain
that he's not the man she married?

BARBRA STREISAND

*E*gotism—usually just
a case of mistaken nonentity.

BARBARA STANWYCK

To attract men, I wear a perfume called New Car Interior.

RITA RUDNER

Childhood is the leading cause
of stress among kids my age.

JANE WAGNER